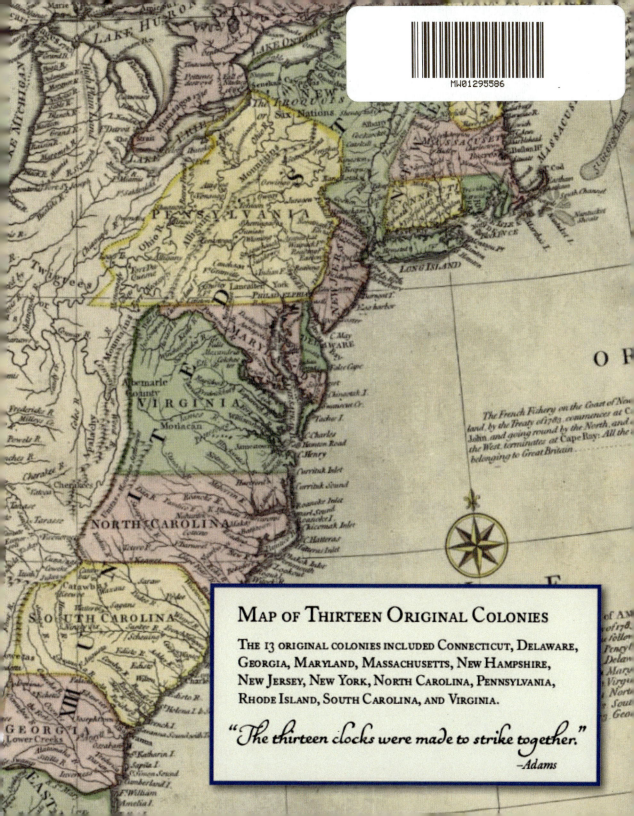

Map of Thirteen Original Colonies

The 13 original colonies included Connecticut, Delaware, Georgia, Maryland, Massachusetts, New Hampshire, New Jersey, New York, North Carolina, Pennsylvania, Rhode Island, South Carolina, and Virginia.

"The thirteen clocks were made to strike together."
—Adams

John Adams: The Voice Heard 'Round the World

"John and Abigail Adams delighted in happy experiments, and they would be doubly pleased by this one. It will inspire anyone, of any age, who loves history and music 'to dare to read, think, speak, and write' in our time, as they did in theirs."

- David Hackett Fischer, Pulitzer Prize Winner, Warren Professor of History, Brandeis University

"This is an important work! It's a great story, I love it!"

- Jean Fritz, award-winning children's book author

"John Adams would be pleased to have his life and accomplishments celebrated in this fashion that brings together history, music and patriotism. John Adams: The Voice Heard 'Round the World captures the spirit and character of one of our nation's most important Founding Fathers. Just as Abigail reminded him to "Remember the Ladies" so this work teaches us to "Remember John Adams."

-William Fowler, Distinguished Professor of History, Northeastern University

"Marian Carlson has created an enchanting, substantive history of John Adams, the driving force behind the Declaration of Independence and second only to George Washington in the founding of America. Richly illustrated with portraits and evocative historical prints, this young people's story is also an invaluable refresher course for adults. As accompaniment to the Boston Landmark Orchestra's charming musical composition, this narrative reminds us that John Adams' strength, wisdom and courage in the face of mortal danger are not dusty historical facts, but the living soul behind 'the voice heard 'round the world.'"

-Diana Rowan Rockefeller, writer, poet, former editor, *The Atlantic*

"...a unique artistic and literary perspective on John Adams, the leading figure of the most important family in American history."

-Howard Gardner
Hobbs Professor of Cognition and Education, Harvard Graduate School of Education

This is the essential chapter in the John Adams story that tells of his vision and courage in making *The Declaration of Independence* happen.

Marked for hanging by King George III, Adams risked his life to secure "Independence Forever" for America. Aided by the strong support of his wife, Abigail, Adams spoke up in the Continental Congress and in Europe with a "Voice Heard 'Round the World."

His dedication to the cause of American freedom kept him separated from his family for ten long years. See and appreciate what John and Abigail accomplished for the benefit of a new, young nation.

Learn to follow the lead of John Adams in daring to *read, think, speak, and write!*

Schoolmaster Press
Cambridge, Massachusetts

Also by Marian Hannah Carlson

Parents, Our First and Lasting Teachers

In Search of the Great American Writers

In Search of the Great English Writers

The Mayflower Mouse

Yankee Doodle's Pen: Wheatley, Washington and Longfellow

American Genius, Henry Wadsworth Longfellow

Available on Amazon, SchoolmasterPress.com and select bookstores.

John Adams:

THE VOICE HEARD 'ROUND THE WORLD

Marian Hannah Carlson

History through Music Series

FREE audiobook narrated by David McCullough

Printed in the United States of America.

SCHOOLMASTER PRESS
993 Memorial Drive, Suite 101, Cambridge, MA 02138

Copyright © 2010, 2020, 2024 by Marian Hannah Carlson

All rights reserved. No part of this book may be used or reproduced by any means, in any form, without the written permission of the publisher.

Original book design and artwort, Dave Brady Art & Design

2024 Edition

Editing, Caroline Lane - CarolineLaneCreative@gmail.com
Publishing Consultant, Haven Books, LLC - MaraPurl@outlook.com
PR & Marketing Consultant, King Communications - JonathaKing1@gmail.com

Publisher's Cataloging-in-Publication
(Provided by Cassidy Cataloguing Services, Inc.)

Names: Carlson, Marian Hannah, author.

Title: John Adams : The Voice Heard 'Round the World / Marian Hannah Carlson.

Description: [Second edition]. | Cambridge, MA : Schoolmaster Press, [2024] | Series: History through music series. | Audience: ages 7 to 14. | Includes bibliographical references. | Summary: The story of John and Abigail Adams and their leading role in obtaining the Declaration of Independence in 1776 and in securing freedom for America over the next 25 years. The last section of the book has pages of places and websites to visit and of activities for young people. The book is also available in a free audio book with narration by David McCullough and music composed by Anthony DiLorenzo and played by the Boston Landmarks Orchestra.--Publisher.

Identifiers: ISBN: 978-0984477678 (paperback) | 978-0984477685 (ebook) | LCCN: 2024911173

Subjects: LCSH: Adams, John, 1735-1826--Juvenile literature. | Adams, Abigail, 1744-1818--Juvenile literature. | United States. Declaration of Independence--Juvenile literature. | United States--History--Revolution, 1775-1783--Juvenile literature. | Young adult literature. | CYAC: Adams, John, 1735-1826. | Adams, Abigail, 1744-1818. | United States. Declaration of Independence. | United States--History--Revolution, 1775-1783. | Young adult literature. | LCGFT: Biographies.

Classification: LCC: E322 | DDC: 973.4/4092--dc23

For Paul, Emma, Charlotte, Elise, Margot, Max, and all those who carry a patriotic spirit of freedom in their hearts.

John Adams, lawyer, statesman, US President, architect of American independence.

Abigail Adams, wife of John Adams, writer, First Lady, mother, patriot leader, homeschooler.

- statues on Quincy Commons, Massachusetts

Hello my fellow patriots!

JOHN QUINCY ADAMS WAS
16 YEARS OLD IN 1783.

I AM JOHN QUINCY ADAMS, oldest son of Abigail and John Adams, the second President of the United States.

ABIGAIL AND JOHN ADAMS HAD THEIR PORTRAITS PAINTED SHORTLY AFTER THEIR MARRIAGE.

I would like to tell you of my parents' part in winning America's independence from Great Britain. My story comes from their letters and through my eyes as a young boy.

You have heard of THOMAS JEFFERSON,
the author of the Declaration of Independence.

THOMAS JEFFERSON WAS ELECTED PRESIDENT AFTER ADAMS.

And you know of GENERAL GEORGE WASHINGTON, our first President. Well, there was one man, perhaps more than any other, who argued, wrote, and spoke up to help America become

GEORGE WASHINGTON SERVED TWO TERMS AS PRESIDENT.

a new nation.

HE WAS JOHN ADAMS.

John Adams fought, not on the battlefields, but by speaking up for America's independence in Congress and overseas. In 1775, Great Britain, with the largest army and navy in the world, expects to crush Washington's army of brave farmers. Thousands leave their plows and pick up their muskets to fight against the Redcoats.

KING GEORGE III OF ENGLAND DEMANDED HIGHER TAXES WITHOUT GIVING THE COLONIES A VOICE IN GOVERNMENT.

Father's words were often called "TREASON."
Some said he was disloyal to the King! His conscience said, *"Shhh, be quiet John! The King will hang you!"* Who was this man who challenged King George III, the biggest bully in the world?

HE WAS MY FATHER.

Our family farm was eight miles south of Boston in Braintree. My wise mother, Abigail, strongly supported my father. I helped with chores, and studied. I can remember playing in the fields with my brothers.

As Father traveled about New England as a lawyer, we kept in touch with letters. Father insisted,

"Let us dare to read, think, speak, and write!"

John Adams was born in this red farmhouse in Braintree, Massachusetts.

The Redcoats attacked Bunker Hill and burned Charlestown.

I was seven years old in 1775 when the war started.

One of my earliest memories is climbing up nearby Penn's Hill in June to watch the Battle of Bunker Hill. Mother and I saw the smoke rising from Charlestown. Over the countryside, the cannons boomed...Louder than the muskets had in Lexington or Concord just two months before! That famous "SHOT heard 'round the world" had marked the war's beginning on April 19, 1775.

"The Patriots scrambled for cover and returned fire!"

General Washington called a War Council to help win the Indians to the Patriots' side. At his headquarters in Cambridge, Washington hosted a dinner including chiefs and warriors of the Caughnawaga (caw-na-WA-ga) Indians in full dress. The chiefs were "wondrous polite and offered their services to the Patriots."

WASHINGTON INTRODUCED ADAMS AS *"one of the Grand Council Fire"*

> The Comtee for Lead and Salt to be fill'd up, and Sulphur added to their Commission.
>
> Money to be sent to the Paymaster, to pay our Debts, and fullfill our Engagements. —
>
> Taxes to be laid and levied, Funds established, New Notes to be given on Interest, for Bills borrowed. —
>
> Treaties of Commerce with F. S. H. D. &c
>
> Declaration of Independency, Declaration of War with the Nation, Cruising on the British Trade, their East India Ships and Sugar Ships.
>
> prevent the Exportation of Silver and Gold

On the long road back to Congress in Philadelphia, Father wrote a list of what needed to be done, including writing a "Declaration of Independency."

He Was Warned To Be Quiet, but Adams declared,

> "...sink or swim, live or die, survive or perish, I am with my country."

Father was brave, but timed his debate carefully. He saw the Congress was divided. Most people were afraid of breaking away from Great Britain. The atmosphere was tense, time was wasting. Father, as the leader of the "True Blue," urged that a complete break was the only way for America.

Had the King already sent a huge fleet across the Atlantic?
Would the King hang everyone involved?
Father had told us always to "Excel."
And now it was his turn.

His conscience said, *"It is time, speak up John!"*

JOHN ADAMS SERVED ON 90 CONGRESSIONAL COMMITTEES AND CHAIRED 25, INCLUDING THE BOARD OF WAR AND ORDNANCE, WHICH OVERSAW THE REVOLUTION.

Father's clear voice filled the hall with "rapid reason." He stood in Congress and stated, "We shall be driven to the necessity of declaring ourselves independent, and treaties to be proposed to foreign powers together with a declaration of independence!" People were beginning to listen.

Abigail Adams was intelligent, patriotic, and brave.

Mother, who was always Father's closest advisor, longed to hear of independence. She wrote to Father about her vision of America:

"...and by the way, in the new code of laws... I desire you remember the ladies."

With Father's Support, Jefferson drafted the...
Declaration of Independence.

The Faulkner mural decorates the Rotunda of The National Archives Building. John Adams is the fifth figure from the right.

"Life, liberty and the pursuit of happiness"

It was a stormy day on July 2, 1776 during the final debate and voting. Surprisingly, many objected to the Declaration, and no one spoke in its defense.

The State House was silent, except for the rain and thunder outside. Father's conscience said, *"Who will speak up, John?"*

Father again made his argument in a positive, reasonable way. Jefferson said he spoke "with a power of thought and expression that moved us from our seats."

Indeed, he was… "the man to whom the country is most indebted."

JOHN ADAMS AND BENJAMIN FRANKLIN REVIEWED JEFFERSON'S FINAL DRAFT OF THE DECLARATION OF INDEPENDENCE

The vote was taken…

None of the thirteen colonies voted against independence! Jefferson gave Father the credit for being there every hour, "fighting for every word."

The Committee of Five presented the Declaration of Independence to the full Congress. John Adams is on the far left in the group of standing men.

All of the 56 delegates signed the declaration of Independence.

"We hold these truths to be self-evident, that all men are created equal."

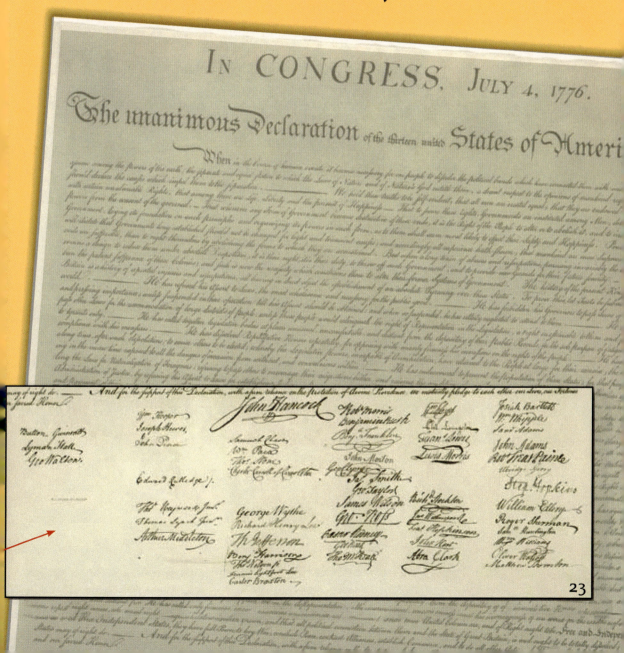

On July 3, 1776, Father wrote to Mother, "my best, dearest, worthiest, wisest friend in this world and all my children."

"Yesterday the greatest Question was decided, which ever was debated in America, and a greater perhaps, never was or will be decided among Men. A Resolution was passed without one dissenting Colony that

... these united Colonies, are, and of right ought to be free and independent States."

"I am apt to believe that it will be celebrated, by succeeding Generations, as the great anniversary Festival...Pomp and Parade with shows, Games, Sports, Guns, Bells, Bonfires and Illuminations from one End of the Continent to the other from this time forward forever more."

ABIGAIL ADAMS WATCHED THE BOSTON CELEBRATION AFTER HEARING THE DECLARATION OF INDEPENDENCE READ FROM THE STATE HOUSE.

A CRY FROM THE BALCONY WAS HEARD...

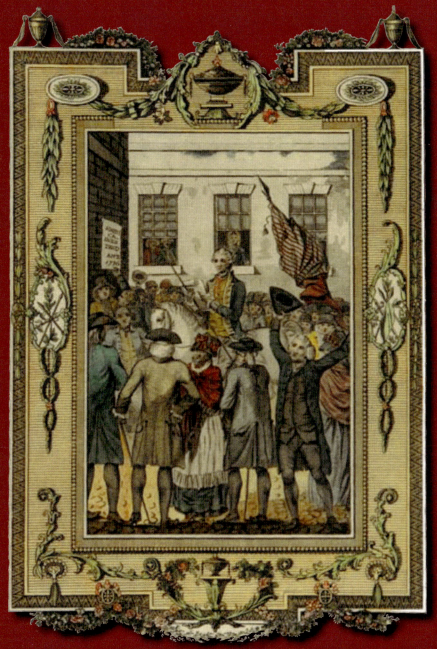

"...GOD SAVE OUR AMERICAN STATES..."

When the Declaration was read aloud in Philadelphia, Father reported that

"The Bells rang all Day and almost all Night.

Even the chimes chimed away."

We hurried to Boston to hear the proclamation read for the first time there. Mother described it well in her letter to Father:

"The troops appeared under Arms and all the inhabitants assembled... when Col. Crafts read...the Proclamation, great attention was given to every word. The Bells rang, the privateers fired...the cannon were discharged...and every face appeared joyful."

The Liberty Bell in Philadelphia rang long and loud.

THE SIGNS OF BRITISH RULE WERE TORN DOWN THROUGHOUT THE COLONIES.

"After dinner the king's [coat of] arms were taken down from the State House and every vestige of him from every place in which it appeared and burnt in king street. Thus ends the royal Authority in this state, and all the people shall say Amen."

Through courage and hard work, John Adams' voice was heard in Braintree, Boston, Philadelphia, Paris, London, and beyond.

John Adams, in court dress of brown velvet, is America's statesman. He holds a scroll representing a treaty and points to a map of America near a globe.

America's Statesman

His voice is still heard 'round the world…

"Independence Forever!"

Famous Flags

The Cambridge or Grand Union flag

was adopted in 1776 and raised in Massachusetts by General George Washington. The 13 stripes represent the colonies. The British Union Jack in the upper left corner represents the hope of peace and unity.

The United States flag

today has 13 stripes for the original 13 states and 50 stars, one for each of today's states.

"I must study politics and war, that my sons may have liberty to study mathematics and philosophy. My sons ought to study mathematics and philosophy... in order to give their children a right to study painting, poetry, music, and architecture..." –Adams

YOUR VOICE!

How do you think about things today?
Do you "dare to read, think, speak, and write"? Don't wait!
The world needs good thinkers and your ideas are important.
Here are some ideas on how you can let your voice be heard –

Read!

"You will never be alone with a poet in your pocket!" -- Adams

Cobblestone Magazine, November 1993. *The Adams Family*.
Cobblestone Magazine, November 2009. *John Adams: Join or Die*.
Peterborough, NH: Cobblestone Publishing.

Gross, Miriam. *John Adams: Patriot, Diplomat, and Statesman*.
New York: Rosen Publishing Group, 2005.

Marcovitz, Hal. *John Adams*. Broomall, PA: Mason Crest Publishers, 2003.

Yoder, Carolyn P. *John Adams, The Writer*. Honesdale,
Pennsylvania: Calkins Creek, 2007.

Think!

Think about how you live at home. Are you an unselfish family member, helping out?
Think about how you can be a better team player. Remember the Rules:
No bragging if you win. No sulking if you lose.
Think about how you can make your school a better place. Are you a good leader?

Speak!

Speak to others with respect and kindness every day.
Speak the truth, even when it's hard. People will remember your honesty.
Speak to others from your heart, without plans to flatter or please.

Write!

Write a patriotic song about Adams or one of your favorite heroes.
Write an editorial letter to your school or town newspaper stating your opinions
on a timely subject.
Write a daily journal and letters to friends and family, as was practiced by the
Adams family for many generations.

John Adams' Timeline

1735	Born in Braintree (now Quincy), Massachusetts on October 30th
1764	Married Abigail Smith
1765	Daughter Abigail Amelia is born
1767	Son John Quincy is born
1768	Daughter Susanna is born
1770	Son Charles is born
1772	Son Thomas Boylston is born
1774	Chosen as a delegate to the First Continental Congress
1775	Chosen as a delegate to the Second Continental Congress
1776	Led Congress to write and sign the Declaration of Independence
1777	Elected as commissioner to France to negotiate a treaty of alliance
1780-82	Obtained recognition of American independence and a large loan from The Netherlands for the fledging nation
1782-83	Served on the commission that negotiated the Treaty of Paris that established peace with Great Britain
1785	Appointed as the first Minister to Great Britain
1789	Elected Vice-President of the United States of America
1792	Re-elected Vice-President
1796	Elected President of the United States of America
1798	Orders the establishment of the Department of the Navy
1826	Dies July 4th and is buried at the First Parish Church, Quincy, Massachusetts

Resources

PLACES TO VISIT

Adams National Historical Park
135 Adams Street
Quincy, MA 02169

Adams National Historical Park Visitor Center Galleria at Presidents Place
1250 Hancock Street
Quincy, MA 02169
www.nps.gov/adam

Independence National Historic Park
599 Market Street
Philadelphia, PA 19106
www.nps.gov/inde

Massachusetts Historical Society *
1154 Boylston Street
Boston, MA 02215
www.masshist.org

Boston National Historic Park
21 Second Avenue
Charlestown, MA 02129
www.nps.gov/bost

Museum of the American Revolution
101 South Third Street
Philadelphia, PA 19106
www.amrevmuseum.org

* The Massachusetts Historical Society's Website presents 1,160 letters written by John and Abigail Adams. Both actual and transcription views of the letters are available.

Resources

MEDIA

John Adams, HBO award-winning miniseries, not rated, but intended for mature audiences. Available from HBO at www.hbo.com/films/johnadams/. Divided into seven parts, it follows the dramatic events in Adams' life beginning with the Boston Massacre.

John and Abigail Adams, from PBS's American Experience, www.pbs.org, tells the story of their remarkable marriage and the turbulent times in which they lived.

1776 is the award-winning Broadway musical that was made into a movie. It brings to life the Patriots during the summer of 1776 with Adams as the central figure. Check your local library or online video source.

ON THE WEB

www.Revolution250.org
This website has a timeline of hundreds of stories from 1761 to 1776 and major 250th events in the Boston area.

www.America250.org
The U.S. Semiquincentennial Commission website is a central location for news about the 250th celebrations occurring throughout the United States.

www.BostonTeaPartyShip.com
Be a part of the famous event that forever changed the course of American history, a multi-sensory experience that includes interactive exhibits, and full-scale replica 18th-century sailing vessels!

https://www.youtube.com/@bostonteaparty250

www.schoolmasterpress.com
www.anthonydilorenzo.com/john-adams-voice-heard
www.landmarksorchestra.org/events/commissions (under year 2008)
For your listening pleasure, an audio book of this book is available for free at these sites.

The Pen is Mightier than the Sword!

ADAMS' POWERFUL PERSUASIVE WRITINGS

In 1765 Adams wrote, "Let us tenderly and kindly cherish, therefore, the means of knowledge. Let us dare to read, think, speak, and write."

"The Revolution was effected before the War commenced. The Revolution was in the minds and hearts of the people."

The Braintree Instructions, September 24, 1765, written by Adams, were sent by the town meeting of Braintree, Massachusetts, to the town's representative at the General Court instructing the representative to oppose the Stamp Act:

"We have always understood it to be a grand and fundamental principle of the constitution, that no freeman should be subject to any tax to which he has not given his own consent, in person or by proxy…We take it clearly, therefore, to be inconsistent with the spirit of the common law, and of the essential fundamental principles of the British constitution, that we should be subject to any tax imposed by the British Parliament; because we are not represented in that assembly in any sense…we never can be slaves."

EXAMPLE OF ADAMS' GRAPHIC ORGANIZER

Opinion/Claim: We oppose the Stamp Act.
Reason 1: No tax without the taxed person giving consent by representation.
Example: We are not represented in the British Parliament in any sense.
Example: It is inconsistent with the British Constitution and with the spirit of the common law.
Reason 2: We never can be slaves.

CREATE YOUR OWN GRAPHIC ORGANIZER

Opinion/Claim:
Reason 1:   Reason 2:
Example: Example:
Example: Example:

Fun Facts

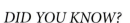

DID YOU KNOW?

A true patriot supports their countrymen! Those who were loyal to the American Revolution of 1775-1783 were called Patriots or True Blue. Men, women, and children risked their lives fighting for liberty and freedom from Great Britain as statesmen, soldiers, spies, messengers, and more.

As a child, John Adams wanted to be a farmer when he grew up. He loved helping his father on the family farm in Quincy. He finally retired from serving as President in 1801 to his beloved Peacefield home where he raised cattle, tended wheat, corn, other crops, and apple orchards.

Adams usually rode his horse from Quincy to Philadelphia and back to represent Massachusetts in the First and Second Continental Congress in 1774-1777. It typically took 13 days in all kinds of weather with stops at inns along the way.

Abigail Adams was known for her intelligence and wit. Patriotic and brave, she not only was John's closest friend and advisor, but she raised a large family, managed the finances, the farm in Quincy, and ran an import business.

In late 1774, training bands of men drilled at night in barns as part of secret military preparations. "The young Men in the Winter months made a Practis of calling on their officers Evenings and going through the Manual Exercise in Barn Flours," wrote one provincial. "I have exercised many a Night With my Mittens on."

Half of the names of our states come from American Indian words. Massachusetts, for example, means "large hill place." Massachusetts is the name of the tribe of Natives who lived near Milton.

Huzzah Patriots Hands~on History Ideas

REMEMBER THE SPIRIT AND COURAGE OF THE PATRIOTS WHO SPARKED INDEPENDENCE!

National and Historic Park Volunteer and Intern
Patriots volunteer to help others! Thousands of men from all 13 colonies enlisted to support the American Revolution. Contact the National Park Service and other historic sites to find good opportunities to help and learn during the summer.

Bookworms
Patriots read and study! John Adams and many others read the Bible and learned many of the basic ideas for American independence from reading books on government by English writers, such as John Locke, and by Roman writers, such as Cicero from 50 BC. Read books about the founding fathers such as Jean Fritz's *Shh! We're Writing the Constitution.* Don't miss David McCullough's *1776* and his Pulitzer Prize-winning biography *John Adams*.

Liberty Tree
Patriots are organized! The Liberty Tree stood in Boston and other towns in the years before the American Revolution. The Sons of Liberty met under the elm to plot and plan independence. Plant a "Liberty Tree" in your yard and decorate it with an American flag on the 4th of July, Independence Day.

Tea Party
Patriots know their rights! The Patriots protested British taxes on tea and other goods they had to pay without representation in the government. Known as the "Boston Tea Party," on the night of December 16, 1773, some Patriots disguised as Indians boarded three ships in Boston Harbor. They quietly dumped valuable tea overboard. Enjoy a "Boston Tea Party" serving hot chocolate!

Victory Garden
Patriots are self-sufficient! In Colonial days, they made their own houses, candles, clothes, and grew their food. The miracle plant was corn. The stalks provided winter feed for cattle; the husks were used to stuff mattresses; and the corn was used in bread, muffins, chowder, and puddings. Plant your own vegetable garden; water it as needed, and watch it grow.

The Quincy Quiz for Young Patriots

CAN YOU SCORE A PERFECT 10?

1. How many British colonies were in America in 1776?

2. What was the biggest goal for the True Blue?

3. Where did Adams meet with the Continental Congress?

4. Who was Adams' closest friend and advisor?

5. Who did Adams nominate to lead the American army?

6. How did the Adams family keep in touch during the Revolution?

7. What number U.S. President was John Adams?

8. Adams said, "Let us dare to read, think, _____ and_____.

9. What famous words did Abigail say during the Revolution?

10. What two words did Adams give the press reporters in 1826 when he was interviewed on the 50th anniversary of the Declaration of Independence?

ANSWERS
No Peeking!

(1. Thirteen 2. Independence and freedom 3. Philadelphia, 4. Abigail Adams 5. George Washington 6. Letters 7. Second 8. Speak and write 9. "I desire you remember the ladies." 10. INDEPENDENCE FOREVER!)

Our Forefathers' Footsteps of Liberty

Proclaim liberty throughout all the land unto all the inhabitants thereof.

Leviticus 25:10
Inscribed on the Liberty Bell

December 16, 1620 • **PILGRIM** families arrived in Plymouth, Massachusetts, from England to begin a new life with religious freedom. All the men signed "The Mayflower Compact" governing themselves with civil laws. Governor William Bradford served 30 years.

December 16, 1773 • The **BOSTON TEA PARTY** brave Patriots openly protested the high British taxes on imported goods and dumped 342 chests of valuable British tea into Boston Harbor.

April 19, 1775 • The **REVOLUTIONARY WAR** began when 700 British Redcoats marched from Boston to capture the colonists' weapons. Paul Revere warned them, and 70 local militia met the soldiers on Lexington Green where someone fired "the shot heard 'round the world."

March 17, 1776 • The **FIRST VICTORY** for General Washington and his army boosted courage to fight for freedom. The Boston Siege ended when Henry Knox transported dozens of heavy cannons from Fort Ticonderoga to Dorchester Heights overlooking Boston Harbor. Celebrated, even now, as **EVACUATION DAY**, 120 British ships sailed away to Nova Scotia and never returned.

March 31, 1776 • **"REMEMBER THE LADIES,"** Abigail Adams wrote to her husband when the Continental Congress established a new Code of Laws. A confident voice for women, she insisted on representation from the men better than their ancestors had done.

Our Forefathers' Footsteps of Liberty

July 4, 1776 • The DECLARATION OF INDEPENDENCE explained to the world why the Thirteen Colonies regarded themselves as independent sovereign states no longer subject to British rule. With the leadership of John Adams, the Second Continental Congress in Philadelphia agreed on and signed the historic Declaration.

October 31, 1781 • The YORKTOWN VICTORY ended the Revolutionary War fighting. General Washington's army, with support from the French navy, surrounded the British under Lord Cornwallis and forced them to surrender. Huzzah!

September 3, 1783 • The TREATY OF PARIS ended the Revolutionary War. John Adams led the committee of three Americans that drew up the peace treaty that gave the United States their freedom from British rule, rights to trade with other countries, and rights to much more land west. America rapidly expanded to the Mississippi River.

September 17, 1787 • The UNITED STATES CONSTITUTION and later the Bill of Rights set forth the supreme laws that govern America today. The Massachusetts Constitution, written by John Adams in 1780, was the main example used in drafting the United States Constitution.

Author's Note

John Adams played a role second only to George Washington in founding America. Besides being the driving force for the Declaration of Independence, Adams continuously served America with wisdom over its first 25 years. As a three-year member of the Continental Congress, Adams nominated Washington to command the American army and then was the head of the Board of War that supported Washington and his troops during the difficult years of 1776 and 1777. For the next five years, Adams was ambassador to France and Holland and helped make them America's allies against Great Britain. He was one of three men who wrote the Treaty of Paris that ended the war in 1783.

After the war, Adams was the first Minister to Great Britain and then served as the first Vice President for eight years under Washington and as the second President of the United States from 1797 to 1801. As President, Adams made sure that America built a strong navy and wisely avoided war with France, which made possible the Louisiana Purchase in 1803. He and Abigail were the first to live in the White House after it was built.

Adams always held to his vision of "Independence Forever!"

The Boston Landmarks Orchestra asked me to write their 2008 commission for young audiences. Already a fan of John Adams, I set to work with a desire to find the essence of Adams and write with an "ear" for the upcoming music. After reading and researching at the National Historic Park, in Quincy, and The Massachusetts Historical Society, it became clear that Adams was indeed the "voice" of the Declaration of Independence, while Jefferson was the "pen." This is a story of courage and wisdom which launched a new nation. May students today be inspired to go on and read more about this remarkable American. I am most grateful to have been a part of this exciting project.

Marian Hannah Carlson
Carlson is a writer and educator who lives in Cambridge, Massachusetts.

Bibliography

Ellis, Joseph. *Passionate Sage: The Character and Legacy of John Adams*. New York: W.W. Norton and Company, 2001.

Hogan, Margaret A. and Taylor, C. James, editors. *My Dearest Friend: Letters of Abigail and John Adams*. Cambridge, Mass.: The Belknap Press of Harvard University Press, 2007.

McCullough, David. *1776*. New York: Simon & Schuster, 2005.

McCullough, David. *John Adams*. New York: Simon & Schuster, 2001.

Russell, Francis. *Adams: An American Dynasty*. New York: American Heritage Publishing Co., Inc., 1976.

Suggested Further Reading

Adler, David, and Adler, Michael. *A Picture Book of John and Abigail Adams.* New York: Holiday House, 2010.

Fritz, Jean. *Can't You Make Them Behave, King George?* New York: Puffin Books, 1996.

Hamburger, Kenneth, Fischer, Joseph, and Gravlin, Steven. *Why America is Free, A History of the Founding of the American Republic 1750-1800.* Washington, D.C.: The Society of the Cincinnati and The Mount Vernon Ladies' Association, 1998.

Longfellow, Henry Wadsworth, illustrated by Rand, Ted. *Paul Revere's Ride.* New York: Puffin Books, 1996.

Silvey, Anita, paintings by Minor, Wendell. *Henry Knox*. New York, Clarion Books, 2010.

Visit SchoolmasterPress.com

Sponsors

With heartfelt gratitude to Willard E. Smucker Foundation and Massachusetts Society of the Cincinnati.

Acknowledgements

With special thanks to the many people who supported and guided this project: Charles Ansbacher, Virginia Hecker, Mary Opanasets, Diana R. Rockefeller, and Bill Nigreen, Boston Landmarks Orchestra; Susan and Reid Wagstaff, Willard E. Smucker Foundation; Warren M. Little, Emily L. Schulz, Ellen McCallister Clark, and Elizabeth Frengel, Society of the Cincinnati; Marianne Peak, Kelly Cobble and Karen Yourell, Adams National Historic Park; Jane Fitzgerald, National Archives; Janet Taylor, Charles Francis Adams Foundation; Mark Edwards, WCRB; Bob Krim, Boston History & Innovation Collaborative; Elaine Grublin, Massachusetts Historical Society; Martha Kennedy, Library of Congress; Emily D'Amour Pardo, Boston Book Festival; Jocelyn Hayes and her Lexington students; Aubrey Cochrane and her Dedham students; Sue Mundell, Joyce Robertson, John Sant'Ambrogio, George Spitzer, Elizabeth Selover, Jean Fritz, George and Martha Moffett, Bebe and Crosby Kemper, and Linda Hennigan; the Carlson family, and many other friends and colleagues.

Image Credits

Courtesy of **The Library of Congress:** Carington Bowles, 1780s world map: **front cover;** Carington Bowles, New pocket map of the United States: **inside front cover;** Declaration of Independence: **4** and **20; Adams National Historical Park,** Quincy, Massachusetts: photos of statues of John Adams and Abigail Adams by Marian Hannah Carlson: **dedication page.** 1775 map of Boston, its environs, and harbour, by Sir Thomas Hyde Page: **11;** American Indian: **12;** John Adams portrait, by Albert Newsom: **15;** "Writing The Declaration of Independence," by J.L.G. Ferris: **21;** King George's Coat of Arms: **28. Adams National Historical Park,** Quincy, Massachusetts: "John Adams" after John Singleton Copley: **front cover, title page, 6** and **8;** "John Quincy Adams," by Schmidt, 1783: **2;** Birthplaces, 1849, by G. Frankenstein: **9;** and "Abigail Adams" by Jane Stuart after Gilbert Stuart, c. 1800: **16. wikimedia.org,** Betsy Ross Flag: **2;** Paul Revere's January 1774 engraving of British ships: **14;** Grand Union Flag and United States Flag: **31.** Courtesy of the **Massachusetts Historical Society:** "Abigail Adams," Portrait, pastel on paper by Benjamin Blyth, ca. 1766: **3;** "John Adams," Portrait, pastel on paper by Benjamin Blyth, ca. 1766: **3;** and John Adams diary 25, February? 1776, Page 7 [memorandum of measures to be pursued in Congress], Original manuscript from Adams Family Papers: **13. National Portrait Gallery, Smithsonian Institution:** "Thomas Jefferson," by Mather Brown, bequest of Charles Francis Adams: **4. White House Historical Association** (White House Collection: **18**): "George Washington," by Rembrandt Peale: **5. The Granger Collection,** New York: "King George III," from the studio of Allan Ramsay: **7;** "Liberty Bell 1776," Lithograph 1876, by Currier and Ives: **27.** ©**Freeskyblue** / Dreamstime.com: A Heap of Wheats: **8.** Reproduced by permission of the **Society of the Cincinnati,** Washington, DC: "View of the Attack on Bunker's hill with the burning of Charles Town, June 17, 1775," engraved by John Lodge after James Miller (London, 1783), The Robert Charles Lawrence Fergusson Collection: **10** and "The manner in which the American colonies declared themselves independent of the King of England," engraved by George Noble after William Hamilton (London 1783): **25.** ©**Clearviewstock** / Dreamstime.com: Old Parchment Paper: **17.** ©**Leigh Prather**/ Dreamstime.com: Quill Pen: **17.** Courtesy of **The National Archives:** Mural of Declaration of Independence by Barry Faulkner, Rotunda, National Archives Building, Washington, DC: **18-19;** William J. Stone Print of the Declaration of Independence, 1823, National Archives and Records Administration, Washington, DC: **23.** Courtesy of **The Architect of the Capitol:** "Declaration of Independence," by John Trumbull, 1817, Rotunda of the US Capitol: **22. freepages.history.rootsweb.ancestry. com:** engraving of Liberty Bell: **26. Lafayette College Art Collection,** Easton, Pennsylvania (Marquis Dorm Collection): "Pulling Down the Statue of King George III at Bowling Green," by W. Walcutt: **28. Harvard University Art Museums:** "John Adams," by John Singleton Copley, 1783, Harvard University Portrait Collection, Bequest of Ward Nicholas Boylston to Harvard College, 1828: **29.** ©**Mozzyb** /Dreamstime.com: Earth: **30.** ©**Anouaras** /Dreamstime.com: Quill Pen: **33.** Courtesy of **Boston Landmarks Orchestra,** Boston Hatch Shell concert: **inside back cover.**

About the Author
Marian Hannah Carlson

Hannah with her son Dave and grandson, Paul, Eagle Scouts who also love American history.

Award-winning writer and educator, Hannah, taught in the Lexington and Newton, Massachusetts, public schools before writing a syndicated newspaper Parent/Child column. With her background in education, she received grants to write for PBS, the Maine Historical Society, the Boston Landmarks Orchestra, and others.

Today, she is the author of high-interest books encouraging students of all ages to know and love American history. She gives talks at museums, libraries, and schools on *The Mayflower Mouse; American Genius: Henry Wadsworth Longfellow*; and on her book and CD, *John Adams: The Voice Heard 'Round the World*. The John Adams "History through Music" project was a collaboration with the Boston Landmarks Orchestra and Pulitzer Prize-winning author, David McCullough, who narrated the story.

Her series, *In Search of the Great American Writers* and *In Search of the Great English Writers,* is the core of the popular Young Writers' Club, enrichment for middle-grade students and homeschoolers nationwide. Other publications include *Parents, Our First and Lasting Teachers, Yankee Doodle's Pen*, and numerous magazine articles.

Some of Hannah's year-round activities include family travel adventures; creative photography; and volunteering at church, local history museums, and historic preservation organizations.

This book was originally commissioned by the Boston Landmarks Orchestra with music composed by Anthony DiLorenzo and narrated by Pulitzer Prize-winner David McCullough.

Founded in 2000 by Conductor Charles Ansbacher, the Boston Landmarks Orchestra is one of only a few professional orchestras in the country whose mission is to perform all free concerts.

History through Music Series

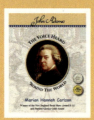

To order
John Adams: The Voice Heard 'Round the World
visit Amazon, your local bookstore, or the publisher.

FREE audiobook narrated by David McCullough

Schoolmaster Press
993 Memorial Drive, Suite 101, Cambridge, MA 02138
carlson@schoolmasterpress.com
www.schoolmasterpress.com